Rueben
versus
Meyer

Rueben versus Meyer

Larry B. Bachman

Rueben versus Meyer

Copyright © 2024 by Larry B. Backman. All rights reserved.

No part of this publication may be reproduced, distributed, or transmitted in any form or by any means, including photocopying, recording, or other electronic or mechanical methods, without the prior written permission of the author, except in the case of brief quotations embodied in critical reviews and certain other noncommercial uses permitted by copyright law.

Printed in the United States of America
ISBN 978-1-64133-956-8 (sc)
ISBN 978-1-64133-957-5 (e)

2024.11.14

This book is printed on acid-free paper.

The contents of this work, including, but not limited to, the accuracy of events, people, and places depicted; opinions expressed; permission to use previously published materials included; and any advice given or actions advocated are solely the responsibility of the author, who assumes all liability for said work and indemnifies the publisher against any claims stemming from publication of the work.

Blue Ink Media Solutions
1111B S Governors Ave
STE 7582 Dover,
DE 19904

www.blueinkmediasolutions.com

Nehemiah 9:17 - But you are a forgiving God, gracious and compassionate, slow to anger and abounding in love. Therefore you did not forsake them.

FORSAKE: *vt.* forgo; leave or abandon

Psalm 42:11 - Why art thou cast down, O my soul? And why art thou disquieted within me? Hope thou in God: for I shall yet praise him, who is the health of my countenance, and my God

DESPAIR: n. loss of hope, lose all hope – despairing *adj.*

Proverbs 3:25-26 - Be not afraid of sudden fear, neither of the desolation of the wicked, when it cometh. For the Lord shall be thy confidence, and shall keep thy foot from being taken.

DESOLATE: *adj.* forsaken; dismal, dreary; forlorn – *vt.* lay waste; devastate – *n.* desolation.

This is a story based on true events which were related to me by Mr. Meyer in the 1980's. The person's name who is the main character has been changed and some creative license has been used through the story line. However the facts are true and the outcome a blessing. **Amen**

Beads of cold sweat outlined Rueben's furrowed brow. Blankly he stared through the rain spattered window glass of the Police cruiser. Hot air blasted from the car's heating system but could not fend off the nerved chill from his body. Wringing his handcuffed hands, Rueben fidgeted to find a more comfortable seating position. The cuffs sent a bleak message of stark reality.

Was this a joke,? What brought Rueben to this dead end? Wasn't there a warning sign somewhere before the worm hole spit him out onto this bridge of sighs? This was no traffic citation; this event should never have been included on Rueben's bucket list.

A canon shot burst like summer's past Fourth of July fireworks echoed the day's events in Rueben's mind. Might there be a get out of jail free card to play? Rueben shuffled his feet, shook his head and looked down at the floor. "Not today", he mumbled, "No, not today."

Despair...

"What's that you say", asked the Trooper in the front seat?

Wrestling with the uncomfortable feeling of imminent doom Rueben replied, "I was just saying that it's been a long day."

"It'll be an even longer night by the time you get booked and tucked away into your new sleeping arrangement", the Trooper stated flatly.

"Hurts like the devil . . . my head is pounding. You guys got any aspirin or something," lamented Rueben? "You could ask the store owner you met earlier tonight. I am sure he's feeling very gracious right about now. After all it was just a can of beans that knocked you flat instead of a bullet from a forty-four", the officer smirked.

That kind remark from the Trooper only increased the heart beat throb of pain coming from the goose egg size bump on the back of his head. Rueben squinted through the window and could see the other officer questioning the store owner.

It was a simple idea Rueben had planned out earlier in the day. He didn't intend to hurt anybody; just walk in the country store at closing time, hopefully nobody around except the old shop keeper, pretend he had a gun and say, "Hand over the cash!" An easy plan, done and out the door.

"But no, that wasn't how it all went down. The old guy had a little more pluck and how'd he know that was just a pointy finger poking at him behind the fabric of Rueben's jacket pocket. How'd he know that? This was so ridiculous, it almost made him laugh.

Continuing on the rewind; yes, he walked right into the store and started doing his robbery thing. Ruben warned the old fellow not to come out from behind the counter but he did it anyway. He didn't think the "rollie-pollie" man would have that much strength when they began to tussle. End caps were knocked over. Groceries went flying off shelves. Finally Rueben got away from the old guy and headed for the door and that's when the lights went out. He didn't know it at the time of unconsciousness, but when he woke up he found out he had been struck out by a fastball; a well aimed 18.5 oz can of baked beans did him in.

A loud grumble came from the officer in the front seat, "Alright . . . hold on fella, lemme' see what I can get out of the store for your headache. Stay put and don't do anything stupid. I don't want to chase after ya a second time and especially not in this downpour!"

> **Psalm 28:7** *The Lord also will be a refuge for the oppressed, a refuge in times of trouble.*

Could good ever come out of this situation? Big-time Rueben brought down by a can of baked beans. The boys on the cell block are gonna love this jailhouse story; "What are you in for kid", they'll question and, "How'd they nab ya", they will ask? They'll all know before he even arrives. Probably they'll scoff and say, "Hey, here comes Mr. Bean the real lean mean bean man . . . he got beaned! Ha! Ha! Ha!

It was just over fifteen hours ago that Rueben was enjoying his daily routine; a stale cup of the prior evenings "Joe" sat before him as he smoked his first cigarette of the day. Nothing new on the early report; same old junk, unemployment at an all time high, bad weather and earthquakes everywhere, people around the globe are sick of social oppression and going to war fighting for their rights. Yeah, everything was normal and upbeat.

"You going out today . . . maybe thinking about going out today", asked his wife? The inquisition continued, "Maybe hit the unemployment office? How about signing up for some assistance . . . I would, but I have a job. The least you could do is try to help out our miserable situation Rueben.

It is all I can do to keep food on the table. Are you even listening to what I say? Turn off that stupid TV!"

"I love you too honey", replied Rueben, and said . . . "it is darn nice to see you're alive and looking so fine this morning!"

"Shut up Rueb . . . stop playing the fool and just try to help out somehow . . . surprise me today and do the right thing . . . okay", his wife called at him over her shoulder as she hurried off to work.

Rueben blinked at the closing of the door. The early morning vitriol interrupted his deep thought. He took another sip of the stale tepid coffee and exclaimed to an empty house, "Don't I always . . . sweetheart, do the right thing?" Exhaling the cigarette's last breath he stubbed it out in the overflowing ashtray and stood up. In his mind he beheld a plan and a smile crossed his lips.

The sound of the opening of the car door reeled Rueben back from the daydream and the officer barked an order, "Look here, I've got some pain killers and the store owner was nice enough to give us a cup of water . . . open up and I'll feed'em to ya."

After swallowing the pills and drinking a few gulps of water Rueben thanked the officer. "There's one more thing too", the Trooper tersely added, "and it is off the chart as far as I am concerned, but the store owner wants to say something to ya. No smart mouth from you either . . . understand . . . the old man seems kind enough and sincere and that's why I'm lettin' it happen. The officer moved away and behind him stood the store owner. Yup, it was the "rollie-pollie" guy who just a few hours earlier Rueben had tried to rob. What a situation he thought, "Did he want to scream at him? Did he want to tell him what a stupid jerk he was? What else could he do?" Suddenly the old man was leaning towards Rueben to speak.

Was it an illusion? Was there a welling of tears in the man's eyes? He spoke, not words of anger, but was it pity . . . or forgiveness? "Son", the man started out, "I'm Mr. Meyer and I just want to say that if you ever need anything all you have to do is ask. If you had come in my store this evening and explained your situation to me I would have helped. If you needed food, I would have filled a cart for you. Whatever was troubling you, together we would have found an . . . answer. It never had to end like this. I would like to be placed on your list for visitation if you would allow. You don't have to answer now, just think about it."

"God bless", were Mr. Meyer's last two words as the door to the police cruiser was shut. "Who is the bigger man now", Rueben wondered, "and who is the tough guy?" The tears Rueben saw in Mr. Meyer's eyes now belonged to him.

"And Jesus wept", Rueben mumbled, "And why now do I remember it. Certainly didn't hear it down at Clancy's bar."

"Why would Jesus weep for me", Rueben wondered out loud. "Why would he even want to?" The one sided conversation continued, "My wife is gonna wonder where I am and when she finds out its d-i-v-o-r-c-e. Ain't never gonna see my kids again. Now I know where I saw 'Jesus Wept' . . . it was in one of those coloring books the kids brought home from church."

Rueben cringed as he remembered what his wife said. At that time she was going out the door headed for church. "Rueben turn-off that stupid TV and come along with us. Times too short . . . someday soon you are going to regret it. You won't ever get these moments back Rueben."

He remembered vividly the looks his kids gave him every time his wife begged him to be a part of some family thing. "Wow, why am I thinking about all this stuff now", Rueben pondered? "Guess now I'll have a whole lotta time to sort things out."

The front doors to the cruiser suddenly opened and the two State Troopers slid into their respective seat. The officer in the passenger side turned and asked, "Is this your' first offense fella?"

"Yeah", Rueben muttered.

"Well, it's not going to be too hard on ya. No priors . . . no use of a handgun . . . just attempted robbery. The man said you two tussled a bit, but he's not even pressing that issue. You are lucky dude", the Trooper summed it up smugly.

"What kind of plan did you have in place . . . what were you thinking", asked the driver, "Or maybe you weren't thinking?"

"Guess there really wasn't much of a plan", Rueben admitted. "My family needed food and I haven't had a job in months. Hearing about it all the time from my wife, I don't feel much like the man anymore. She's got a job and I don't. She provides and I don't. That's it, but it wasn't always that way. Don't take it wrong . . . I know how it sounds, but I ain't feeling sorry for myself. I haven't asked anybody for nothing that's not mine, but for the sake of earning it. Today I guess it all got to me and I fell over the edge. I'm sorry it happened, but here I sit in the back of your fine police car."

"No actually Rueben", the officer corrected, "It's your police car too, this is paid for by your tax dollars and honestly I am on your payroll. I hope that we made you feel right at home and treated you as fair as we possibly could."

Rueben smiled and thought; these two are a real comedy team. He considered that what the trooper said was right. It is true the equipment and the officers were provided by and for the people. There was some irony in that too. Rueben guessed that it was the officer's job to protect the public and Rueben from himself.

And so it went; the arraignment was attended by Mr. Meyer and Rueben's wife. He had not spoken to her since his one gratuitous phone call. The conversation was short and to the point; what had happened and where he ended up. She was oddly quiet. He had asked about the kiddos, but there was silence on her part and then that thunderous click. It could have been considered a million ways within the milliseconds that screamed by as Rueben waited . . . Then listened to the hum of a communication line gone dead.

ℐorsaken... Nervy coldness stalked Rueben again as he shuddered before the judge. This conversation too was brief as the court appointed attorney simply stated no contest to the charge. The sentence was delivered, the gavel came down but there was leniency because it was a first offense. Rueben was thankful for that. As he turned around to share his good fortune his smile faded. His wife had already slipped away. Mr. Meyer was still there and he gave Rueben a smile. Cuffs still in place, the court officer moved him along to be transported to the county jail for a few months.

*D*esolation . . .

Eleven long days passed . . . visitations came without visitors, without incident. Rueben was not happy camping out at the county jail. His home phone was never answered. He had not, nor needed an attorney at this point, so there was no use of any one to speak with on that level. When he was invited to Chapel service he declined. Rueben pretty much kept to himself, even when it was time to mix with the rest of the population.

Then one day . . . "Hey Rueben, you got a visitor", the guard said tapping on his cell door.

"Is it my wife", Rueben anxiously asked the officer?

"No it's some guy . . . name of Meyer I think", said the guard. Then he bluntly asked, "He's on your visit list. You want to take it or not. You got twenty minutes." Rueben put down his hand of solitaire, stood up and shuffled towards the door. "Yeah, I guess, why not."

Going through security was a task in of itself; buzzers buzzed, locks turned, gates drew back and voices on intercoms verified who, what, where and how long.

"Rueben number fifteen", a guard shouted. Rueben went over and sat down at table number fifteen. Yup, it was the man from the grocery store. Mr. Meyer had something in a brown paper bag lying on the table in front of him.

Mr. Meyer was the first to speak, "So Ruben, how are things? But maybe that is a stupid question? How are you holding up under the circumstances? I am honestly concerned. I hope you know that."

Rueben eyed the man, then down at the table and stared at the brown paper bag and answered, "Yeah, I think you are sincere . . . not sure why . . . but I do. Don't think I don't appreciate the visit, I do. It's just that I was hoping to see someone else here before this and they ain't showed up. I guess they think I'm not worth the visit . . . or maybe they plainly wrote me off at this point. But hey, what's in this for you?"

"Nothing's in it for me Rueben, but who are you looking for", asked Meyer?

"My wife and kids", Ruben replied.

"Oh", said Meyer. "I am sorry. That's too bad. You never know, she might have a change of heart. Some things take time. She might be in shock over this business and needs time to think . . . sort it out. You seem to miss them, huh?"

Ruben hesitated and then said, "More than I would have ever thought. I guess you don't know what ya got till it's gone, as they say. Whoever they are?"

> ***Proverbs 16:9*** *A man's heart deviseth his way; but the lord directeth his steps.*

Desolation...

Mr. Meyer smiled and said. "Life can be a funny thing Rueben. It can turn on a dime. What you may think of as an unfortunate turn of events can be a blessing . . . if you look at it the right way."

"Well right now Mr. Meyer", said Rueben, "And looking at it from this side of the glass, it looks pretty dark and I am not too happy about the fix I'm in or my future prospects. I left a lot of people down, but mostly myself. They say if I show good behavior and cooperate I could be out in three months. But man, this will be the longest three months of my life. I could even get out on work release if I had a job or somebody to vouch for me. That ain't never gonna happen.

"Would you mind if I pray for you", asked Mr. Meyer?

"When . . . now . . . right here, in front of these other jail rats", questioned Rueben, looking at Mr. Meyer as if he might be crazy?

"Would you be embarrassed", asked Mr. Meyer and then added, "Even the biggest and meanest character can be brought down by prayer and a little faith. Ever read the story about David and Goliath? No challenge is too big for the Lord Rueben. You need just use a little faith and rest your troubles upon His shoulders for awhile and forget about YOU. And hey . . . I know that's easier said than done."

Rueben thought about the offer for prayer and looked at the brown paper bag. "What's in the bag Mr. Meyer", Rueben enquired?

"It could be the roadmap to a brighter future if you allow it to be", Mr. Meyer said as he pushed the package towards Rueben.

Looking for a nod from the attending guard, the guard retrieved it and handed to Rueben. Opening the bag Rueben removed from it a new King James Bible. He noticed his name had been engraved in gold on the cover.

Rueben was quiet and Mr. Meyer broke the silence, "I know you could have probably used a carton of cigarettes right now, but this is the best I could do and this will help you more in the long haul. Doesn't matter where you start, just get started. Read here a little and there a little and soon you won't be able to put it down. You'll find there is nothing new under the sun and you haven't done any worse than those who are written about in this book . . . probably less. Love the Lord with all your heart Rueben and keep His commandments and treat others as you would want to be treated. That's it in a nutshell."

Rueben looked at Mr. Meyer and Mr. Meyer looked at Rueben. There were tears in Rueben's eyes as he asked, "Would you pray for me now?"

"Now and every day until you get out of here and thereafter", stated Mr. Meyer and added, "You can bank on that Rueben."

Rueben took Mr. Meyers advice and diligently prayed and read the Bible and began the long walk to cleansing his heart. In a few weeks Rueben got out on a work release program offered by a man he didn't even know. Two months later another of Rueben's prayers were answered. His wife surprised him with a visitation. Rueben over tears of joy asked his wife what changed her mind about coming to see him.

Her answer was that she woke up in the middle of the night and thought about him sitting all alone in jail and felt a change of heart.

"Before bringing the children", she asserted, "I wanted to see you face to face." Then she admitted that she also missed him. The one thing she noticed; his eyes reflected the sincerity in his words as he begged her forgiveness.

True to the words he spoke to his wife that time in the visitation room, Rueben remained constant in his daily devotion to God and family. One day after his release from jail, he gathered his wife and children and took a short trip over to Mr. Meyer's country store. When they arrived Mr. Meyer was standing behind the very checkout counter that had divided him and Rueben so many months before.

Puzzled to say the least, Rueben's wife couldn't understand the reason Rueben brought the family so far out in the country to buy groceries. He had never told her until now about the important role Mr. Meyer played in his survival behind bars. Rueben said to his family, "I want to introduce you to my new brother Mr. Meyer who turned my life around and introduced me to our Savior Jesus Christ."

John 14:13-14 *And whatsoever ye shall ask in my name, that will I do, that the Father may be glorified in the Son. If ye ask any thing in my name, I will do it.*

Every day we have a new opportunity to make a difference. Every day we are faced with challenges. It is up to us to make the choice for the good of one another. Human kind is our business and how we fit into the process is our choice.

Treat one another as you would want to be treated and put God first in all you do and say. Amen

---

Trust—Psalm 46: 1-2 God is our refuge and strength, a very present help in trouble. Therefore will not we fear, thought the earth be removed, and though the mountains be carried into the midst of the sea.

CHARITY; THE GIFT OF LOVE FOR ALL MANKIND

1st Corinthians 13:1-13

[1] Though I speak with the tongues of men and of angels, and have no love, I become as sounding brass, or a clanging cymbal. [2] And though I have the gift of prophecy, and understand all life's mysteries, and contain all knowledge; and though I have all faith, so that I could remove mountains, and have not love for my fellow men, still I am nothing. [3] And though I give all my goods to feed the poor, and though I give my body to be burned, and have no love in my heart, it profits me nothing. [4] For love suffers long and is kind; love envies not; love boasts not of itself, is not puffed up. [5] Love does not behave itself unseemly, seeks

not her own, is not easily provoked and thinks no evil. ⁶ Love rejoices not in iniquity but rejoices in the truth. ⁷ Love bears all things, seeks good in all things, hopes all things and endures all things. ⁸ Love never fails: but whether there be prophecies, they shall fail; whether there be tongues, they shall cease; whether there be knowledge, it shall vanish away. ⁹ For we know in part, and we prophecy in part. ¹⁰ But when that which is perfect has come, then that which is in part shall be done away. ¹¹ When I was a child, I spoke like a child, I understood as a child, I thought as a child: but when I became a man, I put away childish things. ¹² For now we see through a glass darkly; but then face to face: now I know myself in part; but then shall I know even also as I am known. ¹³ And now abide in faith, hope and charity, these three; but the greatest of these is love.

www.ingramcontent.com/pod-product-compliance
Lightning Source LLC
Chambersburg PA
CBHW072138070526
44585CB00016B/1738